Teachers

Julie Murray

Abdo
MY COMMUNITY: JOBS
Kids

abdopublishing.com

Published by Abdo Kids, a division of ABDO, PO Box 398166, Minneapolis, Minnesota 55439.
Copyright © 2016 by Abdo Consulting Group, Inc. International copyrights reserved in all countries.
No part of this book may be reproduced in any form without written permission from the publisher.

Printed in the United States of America, North Mankato, Minnesota.

052015

092015

THIS BOOK CONTAINS
RECYCLED MATERIALS

Photo Credits: iStock, Shutterstock

Production Contributors: Teddy Borth, Jennie Forsberg, Grace Hansen

Design Contributors: Candice Keimig, Dorothy Toth

Library of Congress Control Number: 2014958402

Cataloging-in-Publication Data

Murray, Julie.

 Teachers / Julie Murray.

   p. cm. -- (My community: jobs)

ISBN 978-1-62970-917-8

Includes index.

1. Teachers--Juvenile literature.   I. Title.

371.1--dc23

                              2014958402

They teach in classrooms.

They help people learn.

Some teach kids.

Others teach adults.

Some teach reading.

Sam learns to read.

Some teach math.

Emily learns to add.

Some teach art.

Kim likes to paint.

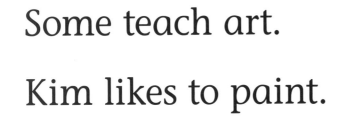

Some teach music.

Tom plays drums.

Teachers work hard.

Computers help.

What does your teacher do?

A Teacher's Tools

computer

tests

markers

textbooks

Glossary

adult
a person who is grown up, like a parent, teacher, or principal.

drums
a musical instrument that is hit with a pair of sticks to make a booming or tapping sound.

classroom
a room in a school where classes are held.

Index

abdokids.com

Use this code to log on to abdokids.com and access crafts, games, videos, and more!

Abdo Kids Code:
MTK9178